Stories of the Heart

Heather Lynn

Presentation by *BookLeaf Publishing*

Web: www.bookleafpub.com

E-mail: info@bookleafpub.com

ISBN: 9789360941284

First edition 2024

TO M... This book is all for you. I shower you with words daily, as they are my love language. Now some of them are captured in a book. All my kisses.

I love you!

ACKNOWLEDGEMENT

I would like to acknowledgment all of those in my life who encourage me to follow my dream as a writer. You know who you are.

PREFACE

Follow the journey of two lovers through a dynamic dance of words that paint a picture of what finding your soulmate in the next lifetime looks like.

I've Known You Before

We meet on a hot sticky night
I have known of your presence
But never have we interacted
Our eyes meet as you hand me the glass of wine

My breath hitches as my heart whispers
I know you
I've known you before
I fight the urge to touch you

We relax into comfortable banter
Your hand wanders to my leg
I've known you before
I lean into your touch

Our laughter fills the night
The wine flows freely
I've known you before
You hold my gaze as we weave stories

The electricity between us crackles
Being with you is as easy as a slipping on an old
sweatshirt
I've known you before

I long to press my lips to yours

Somehow you've managed to find me
After previous lifetimes tore us apart
I've known you before
How could I do anything but fall

Dance

We've danced this dance before
I know your every move
Your body fits inside of me
Just like a tongue and groove

We've danced this dance before
Of this I'm very sure
The way my hand fits in yours
Is something simply pure

We've danced this dance before
Your soul is does know mine
The way we kiss and touch
Is totally divine

We've danced this before
You could easily break my heart
Your stubborn inclination
Was apparent from the start

We've danced this dance before
In this short snippet we call life
The baggage we both carry
Is sure to cause us strife

We've danced this dance before
My best friend, safety, lover
He is my one and only
For me there is no other

Missing You

Missing you feels like an empty space
Inside my heart and soul
Your soft caress, contagious laugh
Make me lose control

Missing you, so far away
Your breath and heartbeat missed
The way your eyes they smile at me
Passion in our kiss

Missing you is distance rendered
Knowing we will last
Loving you is warm and safe
Lives entwined in the past

Missing you is oh so hard
I long to see your face
To see and taste and smell and touch
Please let us close this space

Missing you my one true love
My lover and partner in crime
I know all of your secrets
And you know all of mine

Missing you, this too shall stop
Just like in seasons past
We'll be united once again
Time moving hopefully fast

Sigh

The smell of your skin
The taste of your mouth
The feel of your hands
As they trace the map of my body

The constellation of your freckles
That I know by heart
Cover all of my favorite places
That my lips long to kiss

Your eyes they meet mine
As you slide inside
You capture my sigh
And I bite your lip

I am yours
In every possible way
My heart and soul
They belong to only you

We create the perfect cauldron
Of passion, laughter, and trust
Yet we challenge, questions, and push
The other

To be the best versions of ourselves
I want to be a better woman
You want to be a better man
For the other we accept the challenge

I dream of soft nights
Buried deep in a sea of blankets
Your body pressed next to mine
Quiet snores becoming my lullaby

I dream of lazy mornings
Where you awaken me with a trail of kisses
Coffee in bed and tangled limbs
As we prepare for the day

A life with you
I long to live

Diver

The waves they kiss her toes tonight
Sending messages from the deep
Thinking of her lost love
The sunset makes her weep

For his heart it lies within the sea
Oceans serenades his soul
Diving, exploring the ocean's rim
Her on land and not with him

He lives to swim among the fish
His safety doth she so does wish
That someday though his mind will change
A life with her a great exchange

The diver that she so admires
Promise of passion that never tires
To grow his roots at home in love
Come live a life in the world above

Slip

Sometimes it feels as though he's slipping
Through my fingers
Like sand on a stormy day
Communication and cherished memories
Scattering into the wind
Unable to be resuced

Unexpected twists and turns of life
Create a nightmare roller coaster
Except I don't like rides
They terrify my soul, my inner being
And my mind begs to be released
To the safety of your loving embrace

I cannot compete with broken children
Metal that must be joined
Meeting to attend
Closing eyes and tired bodies
A broken heart that may never fully heal
Letting me encase it with a soft touch

Questions plague my thoughts
Am I enough?
Can I morph into a placid bull?
Will time away crumble this sand castle?

When others are chosen first
Will I not feel the pierce of the knife?

Touching, breathing you is familiar
As though I've held your hand for lifetimes
Yet knowing you, predicting you
I'm always wrong and lose the game
As my thoughts cherished and heard
I don't know

You never do
When you come in last.

Whispers

The softness of the breeze
As I lay awaiting your return
Book in hand
Drink nearby

The waves crash peacefully
I release my breath
Sighing outwardly in learned patience
Knowing you are doing what you love

While you explore beneath
I explore above
Two souls split
For a moment in time

Anticipation of your stories
Adventures with creatures
While my dive
Is into the paper abyss

I know the quiet sooths you
The colors feed your heart
Though worry threatens to engulf me
I trust you will return

Wetsuits
Flippers
Mask
Oxygen

They return and take residence
Once again in their space safe
As you walk through the door
Of our seaside home

Thank You

Thank you for being patient
For intently listening to my heart
For giving me grace when I don't deserve it
For being my best friend

Thank you for tightly holding my hand
For pushing me past my comfort
For catching me when I fall
For telling me to chase my dreams

Thank you for showing me passion
For kissing me soft and slow
For tracing my body with your hands
For making me feel beautiful

Thank you for taking a chance
For going against the odds
For opening up your heart
For choosing love not fear

Thank you for showing me passion
For proving it does exist
For making me believe in forever
For finding me this time around

Thank you for your reluctant communication
For doing what is very hard
For choosing me above all others
For trusting this love we found

Mixed

Do you like it he says
On the phone when we speak
As the picture of the antique comes through

It is old and has stories
That we cannot know
Where will it continue its journey?

The Hoosier cabinet is stately
She sits silently under the dust
Longing to find a home

Do you want it? I ask
It's not my style
Yet I would meld any style for him

The pause is long
I clarify
Would you want it in our someday house?

The silence rings loud and clear
It is not what he meant
I immediately embarrass

My forward thinking

Gets me in trouble
His discomfort is palatable through the phone

Sell it I say
With conviction
Someone will love it someday

Dream

You tell me of your dream
I'm surprised as you never remember
Me in a white dress
Gentry and high of stature

You with your sword
Leading the way
Down the impossibly twisted stairs
Leading me out of harm

Outraged shouting
Arrows flying
My hand in yours
As we sprint to freedom

You're hit and bleeding
An arrow with a fine metal tip
You gasp and your hand wraps around the shaft
Pulling you relieve yourself of the offender

Our eyes meet as blood pours upon the white
silk
Of my dress and my soul
Go you demand
Leave me behind

No I whisper
Sinking down to the earth
Nestling your head in the folds of my skirt
I love you

Kissing your face
Pleading for you to stay
I'll find you in the next life you promise
As you forever close your eyes to the sunset

Stories

I write you a love story
From my heart to yours
You return the gift
From a different perspective

It becomes a game
My most favorite kind
In anticipation
Of how you feel

This venue of words
Is different for you
The one who prefers
To bend metal with his hands

The vernacular is incredible
A powerful mix
Of words entwining
And describing

Emotions too strong
To express
In person
Yet you continue to weave

My morning begins
With a new chapter
To the novel
That is our perfectly imperfect love story

Getaway

Times have been tough
We are both oh so tired
Being miles apart
Is wearing us down

Come home I say
I miss you I need you
There is a surprise awaiting
Time alone in the quiet

We borrow a home that is cozy and quaint
The old stairs welcome us
You are enthralled with the craftmanship
It's perfect you whisper

We explore the bedroom
I can't wait to taste you
In our coupling I break part of the headboard
You laugh and assure me you can fix it

We shower and worship each other
Under the steam
As you wash my hair
Kissing my worries away

Dinner is perfect and we retire back
To our magical oasis
I'm a master at connect four I boast
You beat me every time

Nursing my pride you kiss me with a laugh
I had no idea you were such a stealth
Your daily chess practice
Has come in handy

Try as I might I can't stay awake
As the night engulfs my energy
I fall into slumber upon your chest
Listening to the beat of your heart

Morning arouses me and gives me a glimpse
Of your peaceful sleep
Free of worries and stress
I listen to your breath and kiss your freckles

I tiptoe out to make coffee
Careful to not disturb
You slowly awaken and sigh
In that moment, everything is right with the
world

The Party

From across the room
I catch his eye
He's freaked as hell
And I know why

In a crowded room
Alone he stands
To be my support
And hold my hand

This dream of mine
He did not choose
Yet he still shows up
Even if I lose

Power and politics
Glad hanging galore
Shallow conversations
There's nothing he hates more

We make our way
Through the chaos and crowd
I hear his intimate whisper
Even over the loud

His hand finds my back
Our drinks we both sip
I give his lips a kiss
With a naughty nip

Another introduction
More names to remember
My forever date
Not just this September

The evening wraps up
You made it I say
Slaying anxiety dragons
Wild horses couldn't keep him away.

My rock and my shield
A great team we do make
Unstoppable partners
Which nothing can shake

Taurus Bull

The bull is stubborn
Confident in his ways
Impossible to coax
To your side of the fence

The bull is dependable
A rock for her loved ones
Through thick and thin
She will protect with her horns

The bull is sensual
Fine food and drink
Speak to his heart
A master in the kitchen

The bull is gentle
She patiently creates trust
In children and adults alike
With lessons to teach

The bull is earthbound
Hunting and nature run through his veins
Open land, woody forests, and ocean waters
Make him feel at home

The bull is resilient
Her shattered hopes and dreams
Are swept up and rebuilt
Failure is never an option

The bull ruled by Venus
Governs love, beauty and money
The most sensual sign times two
Is guaranteed to move mountains

Chartreuse

I am the yellow
The sunshine
Burst of energy
And continued conversation

You are the green
The giver
The patient one
Always listening, striving to understand

I am the yellow
The life of the party
Communicating and probing
Everyone is a friend

You are the green
Big crowds bring anxious thoughts
Sweaty palms
And shallow breaths

I am the yellow
Influencer
Big ideas
Quick to respond and argue

You are the green
Conflict is not your wheelhouse
Pondering and reflection
Are your strong suits

I am the yellow
Drawing you out
Challenging your comfortable norms
Making you question your stagnant ways

You are the green
Calming my hysterical ways
Forcing me to slow down
And savor the winning and not the race

As opposites we attract
Shoring up the weakness of the other
The perfect mix
Chartreuse

All of Your Facets

He is Creative
Giving
Patient
Thoughtful

He is stubborn
Unchanging
Quiet
Untrusting

He is Loving
Humorous
Hardworking
Tenacious

He is passionate
Listening
Directive
Assertive

He is a protector
Shield
Sword
Bullet and gun

He is Sarcastic
Shrewd
Ill behaved
When provoked

He is soft
Vulnerable
Loving
Mine

Someday

Someday I will write a best seller
You will create for fun
Someday I will kiss you good morning
Knowing you're my forever one

Someday we'll rock on the porch
Reminiscing about the ride
All we overcame
For me to forever be by your side

Someday you'll wake up beside me
While the sky is quiet and dark
Sweetly making us coffee and biscuits
On my heart you're a permanent mark

Someday a home we will build
Overflowing with laughter and love
Cherishing that you finally found me
I thank daily the heavens above

Someday I'll be your forever
And I will belong to you
With the utmost confident knowledge
That we will happily see our love through

Builder

He built me a coop
When my birds were attacked
As he witnessed
My painful tears fall

He built me a rose
That would never die
Out of intricate copper
And wood

He built me a friendship
With walls of trust
Endless laughter
And such patient love

He built me story
Of love so incredible
That nothing could
Get in the way

He built me a dream
I could not have imagined
Of safety
And passion abounds

He built me a love
That I didn't believe in
Thinking it only existed
In fairytales

He built me a home
Where I wake every morning
To find him
By my side

He built me my dream
Of being loved so deeply
That I knew
We had done this before

Serenades

I am words of affirmation
And physical touch
You are acts of service
In every sense of the word

While you selflessly
Give with your actions
I verbally shower you
With my adoration of words

I wrote you a book
Of poetry to express
What lies in my heart
Wishes and dreams

The dedication is yours
As you hold my whole heart
The honor is yours alone
Welcome to our love story

www.ingramcontent.com/pod-product-compliance
Lightning Source LLC
La Vergne TN
LVHW041246200726
843507LV00013B/2829